Deltas

Deltas
Leonie Rushforth

Leonie Rushforth was born in Ely in 1956. She lives in east London. *Deltas* is her first full collection of poems.

An Irishman flies in from New York to see *Krapp's Last Tape* and falls asleep on someone's shoulder	13
Attendant	14
Recalling First Love	15
In Praise of Salt Water	16
Fontenay	18
Reunion	21
Île Maïre	22
Object Love	23
Pie Bird	24
The Wait	25
Gugong	26
Gorky Park	27
Poplars	29
The Way Things Move	31
Shrew	32
Robert Burton by Folly Bridge	33
As long as it takes	34
Anti-song	35
Here-and-now	37
Little Wind	38
Muntjac	39
I must be going	40
What is really happening	41
Procedure	42

Nest	43
Plage de Normandie, Vierville-sur-Mer	44
Leavetaking	45
Kairos	46
At the lido	47
On Duty	48
How to get there	49
Deathbed	50
Church Farm	51
Delta	53
Through thyme	55

for Simon & Asher

An Irishman flies in from New York to see *Krapp's Last Tape* and falls asleep on someone's shoulder

Up in the steep dark, body heat gathers,
the breathing comes less easily. The wait,
longer than it should be, is long enough
for a few relentless turns of the spool
into what was almost silence,
so that that stranger's lolling head tipping
yearning into wordless sleep awakens
tenderness in the shoulder that will soon
in another several grateful exhalations
receive its bowing.
                            The curtain's line floats
serenely up revealing time unreeling
on an empty desk, a man costive, creaking, choking –
and, while bodies high up there in the dark
begin to remember they cannot bear
themselves either, mysteriously the
stranger's head, naked and still flying over
dazzling arctic wastes, is almost taken
very tenderly in two hands and kissed.

Attendant

Tethered in remote places deep inside
their own time, radio telescopes listen to light.

Such beautiful receivers, constantly adjusting
attitude to align with hope.

Alone in a photograph at a wedding
and not yet three, I'm unwrapping film

in a hotel corridor, looking up
as an astronomer might at numbers

trickling down her screen like salt,
familiar with the indecipherable

and her sceptical attention to what has been
awaited and always missing.

Recalling First Love

There are some who can't remember a face.
Some faces refuse to be seen.

First love is a state of primordial calling.
Pure noise, as when a glacier calves.

In time the lover's spyglass
makes known the bearings of the drifting floe.

The plover enacts a broken wing
to lure the thief. It's an instinct,

a goad. In this way I liked to settle
my debts promptly, debt being so cobwebby –

or you could see it as a choice like this:
to write in couplets of separation.

The dangerous art of the rearview mirror
persuades there's a way to look back

that will deliver us from the future.

In Praise of Salt Water

It's a torment to be close to water, to sweat
on a path above, unable to reach it.

Everything hurts

especially eyes narrowed against
this skewering light rejected by

so many surfaces.

Talk dries up and the island's sounds
depend at first on the scuff of feet and then

the distant knock

of water on rock. No trees, no birds,
undemanding plants inserted into gaps –

you'd think

there might be a lizard or something akin
but there's little life here really,

the white stone's

too good at sloughing off
water and refusing to become earth.

The only thing

is to keep walking, keep looking
for a way down until one appears

and then descend,

gingerly, slipping on loose stones,
following or perhaps conjuring a path.

There's nowhere to change

or hide. It's a paradise! Is it? It's an inferno?
Who cares! Let's take

our clothes off,

slip in by this helpful basin
offering a weedy lip – and let

the water lift.

                We are not all parched
but some who are can almost feel

their thirst is slaked

by salt water, are comforted by the buoyancy
and not having to stand up

any more,

sensors flickering to a different definition
locating limbs in four dimensions

swimming out

Fontenay

one of us can be seen running in slow motion
waving   like a man in a memory

in a suddenly meaningful sunlight
towards the cool gateway where the rest of us wait

the children's upturned faces gleam like moons
pale   pulled in close to the planetary gravities

of parents longing to saunter into the heat
down gravel paths   to be dwarfed

in the austerity of the aisle   reach
the cloister intact

in the church a stone child holds his mother's cloak
cradled in her smile's horizon   an idea

to warm the chill of a communal cell
coherent celibate lives   the aisle is earth

(one of us crouches low   mimes rolling boules)
and leads to a retable where in damaged relief

a pre-revolutionary ox absent-mindedly
eats a baby in a manger   *Death's Door* is open

two of us stand carefully here   under
the keystone between light and shadow

one of us is piping the children
round the sweltering garden where a stranger

will tell them *you'll all go to hell*   swallows
are nesting in the pink ribs of the scriptorium

writing their tireless lines in and out of
the bright door   folding themselves up into nothing

over the lip of the cup of the nest
to feed their safely panic-stricken young

four of us have abstracted themselves
celebrate with illuminated smiles

and upturned faces their *unity*
with the rigorous lines laid down by the authorities

for an hour   recreating childlessness
some of us are celibate   some of us worship mothers

one of us has found his daughter again
he has taken her to look at trout

milling slowly in *the famous hatchery*   fat as monks
who sold the abbey off to Monsieur Hugo

fast when Jacobin fires flickered too close
the forge   *a veritable factory*

is dead   long live the hydraulic hammer
they invented here in the most beautiful room

two of us linger blithely knowing
they won't be left behind   while

in the car park the children catapult
themselves into their parents and yelling like devils

ricochet off to guillotine ants
with the picnic knife   in the long last hours

of an adults' afternoon
running in slow motion to next year's seed.

Reunion

All the rueful nubile angels
on their pedestals, sinking into the soil,
where thorough roots are rearranging
nonconformist bones – all of them
earthbound and disordered
now the paths proliferate what looks like
any how, criss-crossing, leading
astray and soon you're lost where

                    the thought of infants
reunited with the mothers named below them
on tilting stones at the angels' feet
appals then soothes then appals.

Île Maïre

From the east, that is from land and from the shelter of the creek,
all you can see
is shadow, implacable cliff. No landing place,
no purchase.

The only feet over there are cloven hooves that pick their way
on narrow tracks round and
round the enclave, sure and always somewhere they've been before
and very recently.

The strait is narrow too, an 80-metre invitation
to conquer something
despite the signs and sober warnings – *take the currents on! come!
un-isle the isle.*

Professional divers bubble down in pairs to look among the wrecks
of unlucky ships that took
their bearings, as they had to, from this uninhabitable rock
and foundered

and this has been expressed as follows by surface navigators:
5° 20' 5.12" E, 43° 12' 39.84" N
though Julius Caesar's mariners wrote on their maps *immadras*,
that is *mère*, that is Maïre.

Object Love

Six no seven white pots of divers sizes,
not so different from each other, one dimpled
with indeterminate shapes and a little smaller,
another bigger, flared, fluted – each

exerts or expresses, what is it?
not so much a pressure as a purity of longing
for you to need it, love it, become part of it
and you do, you do. Your heart goes out to them.

And I see they will have to go with you
everywhere, even unto the claggy grave.
And here behind the cupboard door
is the too-big scarified brown pot

you have never found a use for but
now you hug it to your unmotherly dugs
and weep into it O humble receptacle
for everything that matters and is holy.

Pie Bird

The kitchen is almost a lean-to affair,
a provisional space claimed from the yard,
clinging to the back of the house as though
a shout might bring it down. The woman

gives nothing away to the watching child.
Her preparations are deft, remote,
the work no mirror. She sets the plums
to simmer on the steady exhalation

of the small blue ring. The purple flesh
swells and splits as she rolls out
the pliant lid of the pie from pastry
she's been cooling in a bowl on the sill

and cuts into it a slit. It flops
over the fruit in an enamelled dish
and over the straining throat of the hollow bird
she's placed just so in the middle. In the oven

the steam won't shatter the crust. The pie
holds its shape and the steam escapes,
forced up, forced out
through the ecstatic yellow beak.

The Wait

For weeks now I've been obedient,
circling the wood's dark matter, gleaning
from the wreckage of the Great Field
the peas that grow harder by the day inside their pods;
I've kept out, peering in from my short midday shadow
through gaps in the guardian hawthorn,
attentive to the presence of absence.

This evening the sweet weight of the hay reels
has been spirited away, the long meadow
at the foot of the wood is as ready as a stage
and I'm loitering
for the owl I'm told will sometimes drift
along the edge as the last light drains
into the poplar leaves.
Whatever happens now –

but nothing happens: or rather, between blinks
distances have been rearranged and everything
has already taken place, dark fallen.
The wood has stepped across the short grass.
The wild service offers its astringent fruit.

Gugong

In the Room for Listening to Pleasant Sounds
I am attentive to the silence.

In the Room for Viewing Beautiful Landscapes
I observe no one is planting rice.

On the Terrace for the Collection of Morning Dew
I reflect on the Chicago trade in water futures.

In the Belvedere of Well Nourished Harmony
I remember *the revolution is not a dinner party.*

In the Hall of the Collection of Complex Clocks
I wait for myself to catch up.

Gorky Park

In Gorky Park
the sky was high
and blue, the crowds
we walked among
were nothing like
the crowds we knew.

On shady gravel
paths we wandered
through a pleasure
ground whose numbered
days turned
round slow,

spellbound,
measured by
the stately Ferris
wheel we rode
above the soviet
city and its river

and down, to watch
our emptied seats
rising to the view
again accompanied
by the distant sound
of fiddles, the notes

of a folk dance
leaping and falling
through the still
unfolding leaves

Poplars

The fields are an ocean of wet grasses.
Cattle steam beside the quiet river
and the forest is a forest that drinks
its fill. The church bell tolls

the slow hours twice. Inside
the manor walls the cedar sieves
the rain, the rain plays with the drooping
fronds while fragile poplars across

the Douix shift and shiver. No
fish rise in the fish pools
to take the grown-lazy flies but
a glass of Crozes-Hermitage suspended

in mid-air
under the stone bridge has claimed
a wasp. The white butterflies pirouette
off to the eaves of the orangery whose inward

cataracted gaze reflects
nothing. Secateurs rust on the shelf.
How many empty terracotta pots?
Green light washes in

through the open windows of a high-
ceilinged room, an impromptu cinema
where *The First Teacher* is learning
his lessons and it is raining too

in Kyrgyzstan, a purifying
drenching roar. It's 19
29. Love
and metaphor cannot rebuild

the school alone: the teacher
takes an axe to the poplar,
the only tree for miles,
and the strokes sing out

across the rocky valley
over the rolling credits
echoing through the house
and down to the stippled river.

The Way Things Move

1   the boat's lurching between ill-matched oars

2   the gnats and their sudden vertical leaps
    inside the stationary swarm

3   the minnows and the synchronised delivery
    of their silver punctuation kit
    in the gold transparency of the river

4   the muscular flick of their disappearance

5   the weeds tugging like flags: the current made visible

6   the high clouds' attenuation or

7   – the tremble between alternatives –

8   the vapour trail's failure to cohere

9   the stillness above the weir

10 the heron's decision

Shrew

echolocator
implacable foe
of white inertia
following his nose
and fierce devotion
to the dark he guards
the golden grain and
curses all that moves
too slow cannot see
what lies ahead but
knows it cannot wait
or come too soon a
long the tunnels of
his inspiration
as he burns burns his
subnivean way to
spring alone each yawn
ing second swallows
twenty heartbeats! how
he shrieks his fears how
vulnerable to
thunder he might die
of fright! through headlong
hours he flees the gape
of day's cathedral

Robert Burton by Folly Bridge
I write of melancholy, by being busy to avoid melancholy

There are those who get their knowledge by books,
he his by melancholising,

though he drowns in what he knows
and has spent his years weakening his eyes

studying at the guttering candle. The company
he keeps is a well-trained company.

When he goes out into the world
it is with what he calls a mixed passion,

walking noisome alleys to the bridge
in search of the bargemen, whose voices throw

him a rope, double him up, haul him
spluttering into the welter of morning.

As long as it takes

You cast me away in the word you can
never remember. It slips from your mind.

It's a coracle made from a snail's shell
and it's the river moving through mist,
blank and bankless.

Slightest of craft, responsive to ripple
and breath, I can adapt – I'll learn
how to cast from a word a line and wait

as long as it takes, long as it's taken.

Anti-song
April – June 2020

The sky delivered a bewildering blue
day after day. The blossom frothed too soon.
We woke in the small hours – startled –
as if we'd dreamed we were lying in crosshairs,
as if now nothing could be taken as read.
Overnight the elderly vanished.
The furniture of home was rearranged.
Predators sold off their holdings in airlines.
Biopharmaceuticals with beautiful names
made landfall. Only the early birds
cottoned on to the cashing out, the cashing in.

The swifts screamed in. New leaves fluttered
in the only crowds. The first rose was ahead
of itself but we the people lagged behind
the frail who were dying in thousands. People wed
to the idea they could take advantage
of the passing hours to better themselves
merely followed the lead of their leaders
whose barefaced intent was to steal a march.
All that was metaphor returned to the body.
Permissions were given. Parties broke out.
The street found itself applauding the dead.

Then the costs were too great to be counted.
Steadfast gatherers of facts lost their minds,
scientists the prize of their innocence.
The troubled exchanged messages at dawn,

like birds. We flocked to the sea. Impunity smirked
at the podium, on the record, in uniform,
on camera, in front of the skull and crossed bones.
News of the decomps was allowed to seep out.
The borders were closed to shore up the fears.
Payrolls were purged, bullies fully insured.
We reeled through June. The roses exploded.

Here-and-now
driving east on the Westway

Oh! massive March moon – your apocalyptic blush,
let me watch you swing in to look closer
at London, this emergency, this rule.

Don't slip so fast behind the scenery, the scaffolds,
the glassy towers – wait! Before you rise steep
into that borrowed glare trite as sixpence

bring me to my senses in this second's splinter where
the office lights are coming on in what can look
like constellations. Nothing must be left behind.

Little Wind
for Rosemary

The rock roses are all of a sudden astir.
Twitching and dipping, they tug
at their moorings.

It's a puzzle how not to think of this
as visitation, as delight –
their fluttering, the fondling

of the fluttering a discovery of petal.
A gold-dusty bee flung clear hovers
in a rivalry of wings.

I'm cold sober awake. I know
the wind is a god, this lover of kistos.

The breeze gleams to the sea and is spray

Muntjac

It was a bitter night. The owl
launched its bookish questions
from the iron gate and mice slowed
their heartbeats almost to stillness. We
held our breath till we emerged into
the mist that drifted round the church all morning
and puffed its way down The Street in muslin cheeks,
humble and strange.

For a few short hours the sun encouraged larks up
up above the vapours to hang
there in a pale blue and cut their notes out
of a suggestion of spring, but on the heath
a stubborn frost held on to the north side
of every rounded mosspad and the distance
was an invitation to step off
that sunny knoll, to skim
the hedges and the copses falling
into the sea and travel mist-wrapped,
incognito, towards the ice caps and
very simply disappear.

The sun reached its unambitious height
and, sinking down
behind the now luminous swathes,
behind the church, the yews, it found a gap
and made a symbol of a muntjac
picking its material way across the paddock,
believing itself to be both spotlit,
as indeed it was, and invisible.

I must be going

The suitcase was left by the door in such a way
as it said: I may not stay

It said: the laws of packing are few
and unnegotiable – first *you*

*trim your need to the space
available*; second *you can replace*

most things; third *order
ensures the flashlight at the border*

does not pause and return.
These laws you must learn.

It said: I am full of the skill or the art
of the fastened heart,

all the disciplined acts of selection,
all the folding protection.

It said: I am fear,
that much is clear

and confessable. I'm the accomplice
proving the provisional and the final analysis

are one and the same.
No one's to blame.

What is really happening

Ships shoulder the quays,
huge gantries slide
containers onto silent decks,
refrigerated trailers gently roar.
Someone knows where everything should go
but there's not a person to be seen.
I am the only soft body here,
on the margin of what is really happening.
The ships move like planets in their courses.
If they make a sound
it's too low to hear
and before I know it they have
already eased away,
their great screws turning
somewhere underneath,
and are becoming smaller,
leaving me blown about
by a salty wind, watching the horizon,
waiting by the indifferent cranes
for the next slow ship to rise.

Procedure

If I may, if I can turn to the language
of poetry, you understood viscera.

You were surgeon and scientist.
That's how I knew your instruction.

No pain, just the shock of intrusion,
as when they pierced

my womb with a needle,
the trembling, the nausea came after.

I learned to watch in the end,
the neatest of cuts disguised as a botch.

You would be flawed, the flake and the spark.
You would be spurned, you would be there.

I would be spurned, I'd still be there.

Nest

O weary angel-I'm-too-sad-to-wrestle,
I confess this once I'd rather
like the mild birds nest or, nearer, nestle,
lie half hidden against another.

Plage de Normandie, Vierville-sur-Mer

We slept to the sound of the incoming tide
as it merged with rain. Soon after dawn I crossed
the haunted shallows to swim, wading past
peaceable sea-birds out to the friendly expanses.

Leavetaking

Rain is falling in a reassuring rush,
a temporary constant. I'm lying down
listening in all my cells. Soothing
as water always is, the reassurance
of this rain lies in the distance
between here and there, me and it –
not far, but far enough.
It baffles the tireless human sonar.
In it there's no emergent shape,
no object. Presence is diffused
through innumerable raindrops,
raindrops without number.

There has been a run of suffocating days.
Last night I woke to see
the curtain billowing up, lifted
by the advent of cooler air. This
is not a sign I thought – the world
has been wiped down for prints.
The rain was on its way is all.
I'm about to take my leave.
Like the rain, you're not far off.

Kairos

Late October and the shadows are long on the beach
where bathers recline under fraying coconut shades.
I'm swiping ineffectually at sand flies
with Kermode's *The Sense of an Ending*,

not quite not here,
our bodies aware of the pulse of the sun,
the small kisses of the persistent flies
and the Russian women in peripheral vision

knitting a conversation across
little distances, one seated on a rock smoking,
a second wrapping thin arms around
herself on her towel, the comfortable third

in her straw hat paddling in the waves,
not quite lost in the fictions and the theories
of the fictions, and aware of the heavy heart
that seems to be slowing to a standstill

in anticipation of the flock of pigeons that skims
in over our shoulders low and fast,
as the fish leap in a shower of commas
out beyond the buoy and suddenly

purple-grey clouds have docked and are pushing
down on the emptied café, the sunbeds,
the young father holding his shining baby
who screams in delight or fear above the water.

At the lido

At the lido steam rises in cold sunshine.

I've forgotten how it was I used
to speak to you when I spoke freely,
knitting you up in the way I see things.

Measuring lengths in a narrow channel
I can feel the terms of your judgment close.

You breathing easier in my absence.

Ineffable anger rose from all surfaces
when we were small.

Mercy is guilt's solvent. Let us not
receive what we say we deserve.

On Duty

My father's burning the leaves. He is dead
but this is the month for the rake
and barrow.

Now he'll set fire to his clothes.
The pile will smoulder for days
untended.

Spreading the ash he'd have found
blackened brass buttons,
knuckly remains of a Father

hollow for flight.

How to get there

The derelict tavern marks the turn. Follow the lane
narrowing all the while and bordered by tall stiff trees,
light-eating conifers, and wonder where the village
begins as the bends conduct you through the fields on the
low road, banks rising on either side, and feel relief
when the church emerges set back on your left, flanked by
the rectory and the modest church room where you find
four elderly people finishing a meeting who
compete to explain the one thing you already know,
the graveyard is not the cemetery, not at all, and
that to find the dissenters you must take the Duddery
all the way to the small crossroads and not (as you did
and have been ruing this long morning) accept the first
invitation that appeared to speak to memory
but led in a wide and empty circle back to the
boarded windows of the tavern – but go on, go on
to the big crossroads, to the edge of what can't rightly
be called a village and turn left past over-tended
houses to find your still doubtful self at what will turn
out to have been Meeting Green though there will be no sign
and soon again another turning you'll resist to
the left that leads away from what has never really
happened towards the rise and half way up, pull over;
park on the verge; step out and to the iron gate secured
by a string easily slipped. Let it swing back. Scan the
windy field. Try to remember where it is and why
you can't remember your way back to the small flat slab,
back to the shock of his name.

Deathbed

She can see the roundel of the bird's eye
fix her from the English sky

Yes she is still
her father's clever daughter

In the long hours
of the night she can hear the soft
comings and goings of her heart, feel the seep
and flood of fluid, hear air
creep into alveoli

When light returns
her children orbit the bed like small
blue planets

Her cares and sorrows
are at last transparent as locust husks drifting
after footfall

She has sucked them dry

Is it May?

The clouds trail an age across the window

She is circumference and centre

It is very strange

Everybody loves her

Church Farm

How not confessing my intent
I went one day to find it,
the house that housed my mother as a child,
alone at the end of a lane, afloat

on a sea of field grass bound
by a moat, a house abandoned but
the door unforced and the steep roof
in good repair keeping out

the weather, brambles massing and pressing,
the smell of fallen soot leaking
from a broken window, letters strewn
across the floor, plates in the rack,

a washing line still strung
between the kitchen and an orchard tree
leafless in May, the hedgerow
unkempt, the moat undredged,

its third side swelling to a pond
patrolled by watchful skimmers and darters,
where a leaning oak lent its shadows
to the water, letting pass

bright shafts of sun that reached
down inside the dark and came
to rest in fiery circles
on last year's leaves and years

before, the rich formless sediment
of hidden life, the layers of a century
and whole centuries before, the house
being so old and steady

where it is, even though
the brambles have set about their work
of demolition and no one lives here
any more, save every evening

your mother taking her fugitive walk
in the long lane and I at last
almost able to make you out
standing at the end of her lengthening shadow.

Delta

Where before the sea a great river splits,
between this arm and that arm, between
the separating slowing courses letting fall
their rich alluvial silt, a delta forms.
Brackish channels of less consequence
than the great crevasses the rivers carve
loop through grasses tall enough to hide
a horse. Among little hummocks
of wind-blown sand, juniper thickets seem
to survive their while on silvery light alone.
Nothing retains its place for long.
Organisms teem, flicker and are gone,
our radical contingency made plain.

The vision of a citadel trembles
in and out of focus in the smoky distance
where the refinery's fat cylinders
glint and its chimneys serve as sundials.
Minuscule ships making for port file
orderly along the horizon's tightrope.
Inland, farmhouses flattened by the sky
keep their counsel and their shutters closed.
You'd think the small black cattle scattered
round about like peppercorns raise themselves.

In geomorphological time, fragments
of stranded river become lagoons
where industrious flamingo flocks
shovel and sieve. White-rimmed salt pans

supply the tables of satellite cities,
simmering into ever deeper shades of pink
as they very slowly flower quartzy petals.
We're standing where the sea once was
and will be relatively soon despite
the locks, canals and sluices
pretending to regulate wilful water.
There is everywhere the evidence
of human ingenuity but one man only
to be seen, far off, achieving
something at snail's pace on a tractor.

Through thyme

At first it appears the brown rock is shifting,
stepping around itself and up the muddle
of glittering scree

and for a disorientated second
I'm as still as the rock that's still there.
But the goat that knows the mountains

is improvising a neat path across
the impossible and suddenly
for an ample moment there are three

brushing through thyme and southernwood
in a silence not a single stone falls into.
Then two. Then

none inhabiting the very nib
of the present as it pushes on
into something not yet lived.

Some of these poems, or versions of them, have appeared in the following publications: *Oxford Poets 2013: An Anthology*; *Test Centre* 8; *PROTOTYPE* 1 & 2; *Morning Star*; *Smiths Knoll*; *Poetry London*.

Thank you to Jess Chandler, Hannah Fussner, Iain Galbraith, Simon Korner, Frances Leviston, Jane Perrott and Andrew Ranken, who did more than help bring this book about.

p   prototype

poetry / prose / interdisciplinary projects / anthologies

Creating new possibilities in the publishing of fiction and poetry through a flexible, interdisciplinary approach and the production of unique and beautiful books.

Prototype is an independent publisher working across genres and disciplines, committed to discovering and sharing work that exists outside the mainstream.

Each publication is unique in its form and presentation, and the aesthetic of each object is considered critical to its production.

Prototype strives to increase audiences for experimental writing, as the home for writers and artists whose work requires a creative vision not offered by mainstream literary publishers.

In its current, evolving form,
Prototype consists of 4 strands of publications:

(type 1 — poetry)
(type 2 — prose)
(type 3 — interdisciplinary projects)
(type 4 — anthologies) including an annual anthology of new work, *PROTOTYPE*.

Deltas by Leonie Rushforth
Published by Prototype in 2022

The right of Leonie Rushforth to be identified as author
of this work has been asserted in accordance with Section 77
of the UK Copyright, Designs and Patents Act 1988.

Copyright © Leonie Rushforth 2022
All rights reserved

No part of this publication may be reproduced, stored
in a retrieval system, or transmitted, in any form or by
any means, electronic, mechanical, photocopying,
recording or otherwise, without the prior permission
of the publishers.

A CIP record for this book is available
from the British Library.

Design by Studio Foss
Typeset in Caslon
Printed in Lithuania by KOPA

ISBN 978-1-913513-21-4

( ) (   )
 p   prototype

(type 1 – poetry)
www.prototypepublishing.co.uk
@prototypepubs

Prototype Publishing
71 Oriel Road
London E9 5SG
UK

ISBN 978-1-913513-21-4